Coke Machine Glow Gordon Downie

VINTAGE CANADA

VINTAGE CANADA EDITION, 2001

Copyright © 2001 by Wiener Art Inc.

All rights reserved under International and Pan-American Copyright Conventions.
Published in Canada by Vintage Canada, a division of Random House of
Canada Limited, in 2001. Distributed by Random House of Canada Limited, Toronto.

Vintage Canada and colophon are registered trademarks of
Random House of Canada Limited.

Canadian Cataloguing in Publication Data
Downie, Gord, 1964–
    Coke machine glow

Poems.
ISBN 0-676-97401-5   ISBN 0-676-97402-3 (book & CD)

I. Title.

PS8557.O843C64 2001   C811'.6   C00-933048-8
PR9199.3.D68C64 2001

Cover and book design: Carmen Dunjko
Photographs: Michael Adamson; Copyright © 2001 Michael Adamson
"Coke" is a registered trademark of The Coca-Cola Company and of Coca-Cola Ltd. in Canada.

Printed and bound in Canada

Visit Random House of Canada Limited's web site: www.randomhouse.ca

10 9 8 7 6 5 4 3 2 1

for my family

contents

how it all works

Sailboat

Can I engage you a while?
Can I tug on your elbow?
Can I steer you a while
my sweet little sailboat?
'Cause after you've looked into
the half-lidded eyes of the wicked
the most you can do
is roll with the waves
gently kicking.
Evanesce fade disappear
into a world easier on dreamers
where the tide's escaping
leaving a lunar landscape with puddles
reflecting the real moon
as a water balloon
parallax and misshapen.
Coalesce stay reappear
in a world
easier for dreaming
where sun showers turn the good road
into bands of silver
and blue sky reflected in chrome
is vaguely familiar
in a world
easier for dreaming
where the most you can do is
spend all your time
giving some of your time
meaning.

Kieteldood
(death by tickling)

If the music's right
monarchs descend
in freckled elegant
moonlight.
To the
Paradiso
to the dark purple pudding skin
of your bare shoulder
and in drowsy multitudes
cling to the soul
slowly blinking wings
eyelashes lightly
batting
on my cheek;
sex lined with butterflies
and the story unfolds
if the music's right
you'll whisper,
"This is
Kieteldood."

Trick Rider
(for C.)

My wild child, your night light's on.
You're in your mild depths,
the moon is on the lawn.
Just make your friends
while you're still young,
before you can't see
through anyone.
And if you're trick-riding out in the rain,
don't expect me to watch
and don't ask me to explain.
I'll be your friend, your last refuge
when things get weird
and weird breaks huge.
I'll stroke your hair,
I'll dry your cheeks
when the failures come
and no one speaks,
but if you're on a horse,
trick-riding in the rain,
don't make me watch,
don't ask me to explain.
If you're trick-riding
out in the mud and rain,
you can't expect me to watch
or ask me to explain.

Toboggan Hill

I'm thinking back to when we were young
and eating donuts
with a set of plastic vampire teeth
that we were passing back and forth.
We weren't so young as to
think a dog was a horse.
Nor were we old enough yet to name
the cold purpose of musical chairs.
We were like-minded spirits
ekeing out a rhythm
whispering transmissions
through wet woollen mittens.
Growing up on a toboggan hill
nothing was material.

I'm thinking back to when we were young
if only to find out
forensically
what it was
we used to
want.

Summer On

There's fragrance before the storm.
I know it's June because there are kids laughing
in the night at nothing for no reason
and your skin's so soft I can barely tell I'm touching it.
The sound of a thirsty dog
drinking down the hall finally
interrupts us—
Oh yeah, and the storm;
clouds full of dimes
threaten the dream
and the dream's architect.

People are becoming their essence
and the calm is verging on excessive.

She Could Be Her Mother

In the morning I answer drowsy entreaties;
I go upstairs.
The mood is tender and lacks latitude.
"Let's get some air in here," I offer.
"Let's let some light on the sitch-ee-ay-shun."
She could be her mother when she says,
"I want company, not light."

Wow Not Wow

Rain on the truck stop
Puddles on the parking lot
Sunshine on the clouds
Random in a sky
of spilled paintwater.

Wow not wow
you said
in a gulp of swallows.

W's Mind

I have a secret.
Tell me.
No.
Please tell me.
No. Put it out of your mind.
Please? If I put it out of my mind, then will you tell me?

My Girl

Grumpy ballerina in her rug routine
showing her fantastic basket
and her strawberry crate.
This is what my genes
have been waiting for.
A female host.

The Goalie Who Lives Across the Street

Jean Beliveau's welcome any time
at the outdoor rink
in the park
just across from my house
for morning hockey under blue skies this winter.
Birds wheeling overhead
Russian temperatures
lousy to no gear.
I'm The Goalie Who Lives Across the Street.

Kids play with smokes hanging out
of their mouths;
beautiful puck hogs
with incredible tricks.
They are so easily fatigued,
they take a break after every rush.
Old-timers heckle:
"Hey, Jim Carroll. Pass the puck."
They don't get it.

No literary pretensions allowed.
Two minutes for
"I saw his blood,
a billowing crimson cloud
against the milk white ice."
That's an infraction here.

When the predatory follow the puck down to the other end
my net swarms like the Great Barrier Reef
with the smaller fish.
My crease fills with good questions
and wobbly wrist shots
(there are no bad questions, only bad wrist shots).

And then there are
the parents
always yelling
always telling them
where to aim.

At the rink across the street
Gerry Cheevers is welcome any time.

How It All Works

The moon's a lime
turning around the earth tonight,
being played by a tomato.
The sun is a honeydew melon.
I have only two hands,
so you hold the melon,
er, I mean the sun, and
I'll show you how it all works.

Peach

We're getting sick of the stars
and the constant reinvention
of the peach.
And now that we can reach
each other
we don't know when we'll see
each other
again.
Let's be
like everybody else:
not a furnace to be fed
not a cow barn to be mucked out.
Let's die
with our secrets.

Old Note

"Soothers, hair elastics, tube socks, panties and pads."
A note in the kitchen that now seems
overwhelmingly sad.

Some Days the World Can Be the Greatest Place on Earth

I'm off on the second,
I'll be unrecognizable after that,
I have you to thank for this time
and your sisters before you
and your mother before them.
I live with architects
architects who designed
this perfect life.
But it's time for the grand unravelling
for the great confession to begin
for the sacrificial ideal
to hit the good Catholic road.
Please don't cry, little architect.
If you start to cry
you'll make me cry
and, believe me, my crying
could make your crying
look like laughing.

Insomniacs of the World, Good Night

I can see the line of your brassiere.
I can contemplate it from here.
There's no need for breathlessness
when we're so far apart.
I see us writhing in a phone booth
or laid back in the dewy grass of our youth
and gathering our sweetnesses
and wishing on the Neverstar.
And happy days of electrical smiles
and loving evenings falling down in piles
and not imagining a restlessness
that could keep us apart.
If I could sleep there's a chance I could dream
and reconjure all of these vivid scenes.
O insomniacs of the world, good night.
No more wishing on the Neverstar.

Art vs. Commerce

Paternity leave from a rock 'n' roll band.

a drop of audience

Clouds

I'm trying to find my house on the ground that's
rapidly falling away.
Clouds are complicating things.
The jet climbs into life after death
towards that place where all the longing goes.
Asides turn integral
and what was once freely given
is now gotten by force.
We move into the pitiable stage. The silent phase.
With the loyalty of a doper
and the unerring purpose
of some future poet's dad
pushing a hot dog cart up Fifth Avenue,
the jet has decided to stay
in the air. Today.

Starpainters

The myth is neither here nor there,
from the air.
Just blue lake stains
on green and purified, parcelled squares:
a crazy quilt of spearmint,
of mustard and honey tones;
a scuffed-up kitchen floor of tiles
on top of bones
with a big trap door.
Towns down diagonal lines disappear
and drop out of sight
into the night beyond the national night,
and underneath the grit and glare
into unfettered nothingness and thin air,
as herds of clouds lazily graze
on thermal sighs of delight.
The Starpainters are taking over now,
their scaffolding is in its place.
Your anaesthesiologist tonight
is washing up and on her way.

I Stand Before the Songwriters' Cabal

I stand before the Songwriters' Cabal,
bearing gifts of drugs and alcohol.
They say, "That's not enough and that's not all
and go stand over there 'til your number is called."
O I'll step up to the mic and sing
voice tinkling like a chandelier
'til god or a reasonable facsimile appears.

Called before the Songwriters' Cabal,
wide-eyed just to be included in all this
exuding of warmth to the point
when a voice, at once calming and benign,
that's soothed the soul every time after time,
like a barré chord swiped down the register line,
says, "Don't invent a demand in your mind.
And don't tell them more now than they believe.
Don't tell them what they've already heard.
Don't describe the footsteps you've taken
or the horizon you serve."

I stepped up to the mic and sang
voice tinkling like a chandelier
when god or a reasonable facsimile appeared.
I sang, "Don't Tell Us More Than We Believe"
and "Don't Tell Us What We've Already Heard."
I sang, "Don't Describe Your Footsteps,
and The Horizon You Serve."

I'm Not Sure What Kind of Squalor You're Living In

In a small town with no therapy
just confession
you never apologize for anything
that means anything.
Consumed with reconciliation
I leave my weirdest song 'til the end
"I'm Not Sure What Kind of Squalor You're Living In."

In the big city with just therapy
there is no confession
you're sorry for everything
and it means nothing.
Consumed with show business
I leave 'em wanting more.
"I'm Not Sure What Kind of Squalor You're Living In."
Thank you.
Good night.

The Michigan Suite
(for W.)

To Michigan
the most American of states
I've heard they can take your temperature there
and turn it into white noise
with big American air conditioners
that condition the sound of your air
into a beautiful heavy industry.

Michigan Roadside

I'm a van full of balloons
by the side of the road.
Everything's moving but me
the target desirable, unguarded.
I'm an abandoned dog
a broken ball, half full of water
rocking in place.
Inches from the howling
parallel dimension
a swift cautery
a cascading roar
a vehicular torrent:
the commuter tsunami
of Michigan
achieving mean speed.

Michigan Gig

"Tyranny of idiots," I mutter,
"my songs were built to fight wars."

"Is there anybody out there tonight
who's seen this before?
If you have, don't say anything…"

I stood there before them
all stem and goblet,
lips full of wine
a glass designed to fight wars
a General among singers.

Lowell, Mass.

It's cold tonight
in Lowell, Massachusetts.
It's making for more enhanced hearing
among the vice-ridden and the retired
who know a thing or two about
conductive loss.
You get the sense
on a heavily doctored night like this
that in a dream mistaken for prescience
even Kerouac would convert you like a Huron if he could
and get you to say what words can't express:
that powerlessness
with a mathematical bent
colours commentary
into local anaesthetic.

The Band, Upstate

We talked our way through the Catskills
earning rides with a Richard Manuel-ease:
a weird polite that is our birthright.
We built stilts for our private conversations,
kept our words in the trees
when we slept
under rickety scaffolding,
Thanksgiving sticking to everything
and fall madness falling constantly.
We huddled with cows for warmth
by the reflective surface
of a tin shed
sucking the last of the sun
from the west.
A cat coaxed some milk from
an ice-cold udder
with a certain
Danko-esque charm.
What a cat.
They should all be so loved.

A Drop of Audience

A drop of audience
gets you songs with a view

and in a
burst of Florida
it gets you past the politics
to the blank dolls.

Drink
until your face falls.
When the water's all gone
and you've wrung your notebook dry
leave the stage
behind the audience's back.

New Orleans

In 20-watt New Orleans
envelopes lick themselves.

Das Beauty

I named my guitar
My Beautiful the Whore.
Everybody's coughing here.
And music's infiltrating work
in the most pleasant way.
It's a system based on silver
where listening's an extrasensory perception
and talking's the only psychic thing
and I can dress you in my thoughts
until you wear them.

I've been taking care of my clothes
Like they're cattle.
(Try this shirt
it would look so good on you.)

Heavy Rotation

The moon's so beautiful
when you show it to me.
That's the song playing
on my inner stereo
around the clock.

Earth Diva

With just a hint of Goldie
she put the "L" back in folk music.
"This is like taking candy from 17 babies,"
she let slip
in a proclamation from Mt. Stage.
I love you all so much
I could eat you on toast.
She got so big
that every time I sang
only her voice came out.

Who by Rote

As neutral as snow
covering up violence
your mind was smashing its gear
like the Who by rote
at good ol' Monterey
(where some people cheered
and some looked away).
Your best words
the most
economical and
clear to the ear
nullified and kept
by mum protectors
of a suicide note.
But the best part of cold
is that faraway is close.
The distant bark of a
lone snow shovel
digging out after the storm
is a rhythmic whisper:
"I'm here because you're here.
When you go
I'm going too."

Coke Machine Glow

Here we are on the highway.
Here we are on the road.
Here we are in the parking lot's
pink Coke machine glow.
Here we are in the bedroom.
Here we are in the bed.
Here we are
beside each other
after everything
we've said.

My Road Diet

Beer and gum.

Rochester Hotel Bar

There's horse-racing on TV.
The bartender leaves off picking dirt
out of her beautiful fingernails
and switches it to golf.
The working couple
working drunkenly beside me
are talking loudly
(about their work).
"Don't talk in whispers—nothing's more conspicuous,"
she says (loudly),
and "If it ain't negotiable, it's shit" (softly),
over and over again.
He's writing off checkmarks
and crossing out tasks
with a slurred flourish.
She's telling him what to say to his cellphone.
It's all getting so hot.
Golf music swells.
They slip away.
"We're just going upstairs"
to make competitive sex
and ocean smells.
The bartender returns
to her beautiful
dirty fingernails
and
horse-racing
on TV.

Minneapolis Hotel Room

Here I sit
cool as a garage
writing by lightning.
I don't mean lightning as metaphor for inspiration
I mean lighting
intermittent lightening
by lightning
really turning it on.
A lightning-powered hotel room.
It's the most lightning I've ever seen
in one room.

Syracuse—University Tower Hotel

The mouthpiece of my phone
reeks of rambling
Aqua Velva business
and flirting skills
of the razor widening its scope
"I need more room to move,
more time to manoeuvre," I said.
That's what everyone says into this phone.
It's strictly for pleading
(75 cents per call).

There's radiation in the drapes and out the window
various and sundry states of decay
the Great Extramural Interstate lurching with flow
gullivering the city
rattling pipes and flaking red-brick paint.
Great Tourniquetted Interstate
bracketed to the midriff
of this cored hotel since 1968.

Fingerprints swerve into scrawls on the window,
gooey smudges of a child
marking a transitory stage?
Sex against the window
for the pleasure of the Interstate?

SF Song (San Francisco/The Phoenix Hotel)

I think it was the click-click-clicking of the fingernail clippers.
Or was it the sound of laughter outside?
Or the pad-pad-padding of the chambermaid's slippers?
But I'm awake. I'm awake.
"I'm awake and quite aware of checkout time."
Out and down past those stickers
on that chambermaid's cart.
Past the suits with wet hair at the breakfast buffet.
Through the lobby where the World's Largest Lemonade Stand
starts off each day by shooing away a guy with a sign that says,
"I'm saving up for a harmonica one day."
And past the girl in the wheelchair who says,
"It's not mine, I'm just sitting in it for someone."
And just then there's a bus with a Marlboro ad on the back that says,
"Bob, I Miss My Lung," except it says,
"I Miss My Lung, Bob."
It's 'cause I paraphrase so much,
but I think it was "I Miss My Lung Bob."
You know, I think it was;
I think it was.

Toiletten

Hitler's podium at Nuremberg
now points the way
to the Toiletten
it's a sign
rendered ridiculous by time
that tourists get behind
to do their best imitations
of heavy
then they leave it
to its long shadow
and the
skinny
imminent
night.

Storm Over Rochester

I'm Hotel Invisible
reflecting dark clouds
behind my window.
Strong heavy winds
throw rain
clearing the poolside deck.
Just beyond the pool
the brown Genesee River
is eddying all casualties and reinventions
through the makeshift flumes
of the Sister Cities Bridge.
It's heading off to break the States
on the backs of the accident-prone
brusque, distracted, tough
whispering a word that's never enough
rolling it over on the tongue
a word for erosion:
"inconspicuous"
"inconspicuous"
"inconspicuous"

The Vegas Strip

Black dogs sense a foundling
and start surrounding
smacking their lips
but you lit up
their darkest deep bonhomie
like the Vegas Strip.

Black thoughts drug dominions
and choke opinion
in diaphanous grip
but you lit up
the narcotic routes
of nocturnal brutes
like the Vegas Strip.

Equitone
(for Dan Gibson)

Shhhh.
A most acceptable wind
has urged and nurtured a wave
all the way from Japan
with a silvered crest
to say its peace
in a rush.

A rustle doesn't have a place
in this "bombardment of aloneness."
Shhhhh.
Is that all?
Is that it?
Shhhh?

No Stopping Inmates Working

"I'd like to spill that in my computer"
and "Hey, blondie, drop your laundry"
came from the construction site
as you walked by
so proud of your destination
sending things astir.

O just to stop
this concerted traipsing
and follow
your ponytail home
settle down
in the crook of your knee
and blow on your tiny nails
until the polish
dries.

Tuba

If I was your tuba
you'd take me everywhere.
I'd be designed to
make you smile.

Glowing Bamboo

Writing with fingers of glowing bamboo.
I'd like you to see what's inside me:
attraction to living things
explosions in the narrows
splendid isolation.
I'd like to have last night's
phone call
annulled.

I Wonder What I Thought I'd Do

I was cruising through fall's Falling Colour Cruise
through walls of dope
and apartment stew
past Shangri-La and Malibu
Sobaki and Gaë-Wolf too
to Mariana's Trench
to get a sprig of mint for you.
I wondered what I thought I'd do
when the best things about you
are the lengths you'll let me go to.
When the best things about you
are the things I can't see, can't hear
but want to.
I wonder what I thought I'd do.

My Name is Figment

My name is Figment.
I'm not who you think I am.
All my heroes are women
and all those women are cinnamon.
Even though the sanding sound
of grudge on the collective
leaves a pile of puzzle dust
and me cake-drunk, crying,
"What has happened to us?"
I still feel that as long as we're talking in drift nets
and as long as we swim swim swim
and hold hands in the swiftness
of all three dimensions
that on the road without perspective
if there's a rotation afoot
the things we come up with
will still be
surprisingly put.

every irrelevance

Every Irrelevance
(for Chi-lin)

There's no sound so profound
it can't even be heard.
No silence or violence
that can't be disturbed.
So just say it, convey it,
sing out like a bird.
If it's secret, I'll keep it.
I give you my word.
Even though I know
it don't make any sense,
I'm in love with your every irrelevance.
Catharsis?
My arse is capable of more flush.
And exposure
just for "closure" won't accomplish much.
And if these loose words go unheard,
what's it matter to us,
because we're friends
and in essence, it's all about trust.
And all at once
life's richness and consequence
was there in your every irrelevance.
Even though I know it don't make any sense,
I'm in love with your every irrelevance.

Gift Advice

What do you give
the woman
who gives
everything?
More attention than Cleopatra?
Your tongue to the hilt?
A shot o' Yeats?
A sixth sense? (The Ampullae of Lorenzini?)
A cookie factory?
A frozen tiger lily?
A power envelope?
A heart as big as Merton's Heart?
A moonlight fuck?
An incendiary device?
An antidote for ecstasy?
A basting syringe?
A sceptical sigh?
Stock mannerisms?
A showering of generosity that could serve
only to make her loathe you?
Future songs?
Wonderment giving way to delays?
Quintuplets?
Atlantic realism?

L. vs. Al

The baby sleeps fitfully
as I gently turn the pages of *The Cariboo Horses.*
These pages are as old as I am
and make hissing sounds as they're turned;
tiny parched
dry explosions of relief
audible only to
readers and babies.
His eyelids flicker.
Maybe he's writing
"Why read old poetry
when improvisation's as 'in'
as a volcano?"

Is it the crinkling of these 36-year-old pages
that disturbs?
Or is it maybe the smell
as unique the other way
as baby smell?
Perhaps the womb
smells like an old book
and when released
longing for the hunt
we retrace our steps
to that most sodden place
with dry memories of total comfort.

I walk the floor
child in one arm
Al Purdy in the other.

Both have innate knowledge
of hereditary jealousy
and the envy machines
where everything goes in
and nothing comes out
but a puff of smoke.
Perhaps even the tiniest noses
are trained to sniff
for bombs
of wistfulness.
Whatever the reason
he stirs and grunts
so poised to rage
I can't get through a single poem.

I'm sure
they both know
it's the old things
you've got to
destroy first.

We're Hardcore

We're not hobbyists
or dabblers any more
we're hardcore
hardcore
we're hardcore
there's a kid in the street
one up in bed
one on the hip
one on the floor
we might be one again
but not like before
we're hardcore.

Chancellor

Seconds from pajamas I must first open all the doors
and the windows
and invite the vampire in to be one of us.
Then, in the guise of cool air, in the softer hours,
he's there, sitting, talking
in the voice of your mother
about leaving one good party for another
and the night of a thousand missteps
and the loss that made him dogged
or it could've been the doggedness
that caused the loss in the first place, I guess.
Crazy daisies and wooden stars,
the threat of oxygen on Mars,
marching armies in the night,
smiling strangers riding by on bikes.
Children smoking, sloganeers on mics,
just a few things most vampires don't like.
Before the dawning's first light
I must first close up all the doors and the windows
and try to trap that cool air to be one with us.

I'm discovering uses for you I thought I'd never find.
I could've made chancellor without you on my mind.

Run the Barrens

Here in the Stimulation Department
the squirrelliest-sounding stuff
gets seriously curtailed and
the last eyelid closes
at around 10 p.m.
That's the junction
where dreamers beginning to write
pass writers beginning to dream
running the Barrens.

This Empty House

I'm writing this on the back of the carbon-monoxide detector,
the last thing of ours to leave this empty house.
Our stains on the wall stay.
Our dusty lines and puke traces,
under where the crib used to be, stay.
The waste of a thousand true projections,
behind where our mirrors were, stays.
The smudges of our children's peregrinations
around their beds, looking for clearer,
cooler needs in hospitable cracks,
stay on the walls I painted
the last time this house was empty.
Go down the stairs, lock the windows, pull the blinds
leave the main chandelier glowing
and the hydro bill behind,
slam the door.
The knocker knocks its first knock
for other people.

The Never-Ending Present

This waiting here for a bus is
almost better than its coming.
Every day it always does
as I daydream or kick some dirt
or throw a rock or check my watch
or catch my reflection.
And it barely makes an impression
in the never-ending present.
This working from the inside out,
this stepping to the easel,
is gonna run you into results,
then there's the materials:
to see a world beyond your shoes
reflected in the polish and see some images
of truth beautifully demolished.
And it barely makes an impression
on the never-ending present.
Steel yourself against the cold
or look for semi-precious shade.

When the bus crests that hill,
love and hate are just the same.
Watching as the money drops,
every day it always does.
Maybe there's a song in here.
No, and in fact, there never was.
Just a little expression
in the never-ending present.
Just me doing my impression
of the never-ending present.

Air Show

High above, the Snowbirds are regrouping for another pass.
My dad loved the air show. "Though," he always said,
"it's a bit like bringing a cannon to a pea-shooter fight."
I think about him every time a shaky telephoto jet slams
into the aluminum lake amid the merrily bobbing pleasure craft,
every time a dependable jet turns into a flaming mosaic
of exploding octopus parts and billowing orange ink
in full view of the grandstand
covering its eyes and plugging its ears,
rocking and chanting,
"This will not be an abstract experience…This will not be an abstract
experience…This will not be an abstract—"
I always think of my dad somewhere thinking,
Surely, this will be the end of the air show.
High above, the Snowbirds are taciturn
wing tip to wing tip
a poodle-length apart
regrouping for another
engravable pass.

Granddad

There's a haunting picture of you and a horse
You were never in better shape than you were
In World War II
Skinny little sinews
You were so tenuously you
This horse for Churchill.

Lofty Pines (NYC)

It's too hot to sleep. Let's gather 'round the fan.
We can't do nothin' 'bout the heat,
so let's just do what we can
and everything'll be just fine.
Just dream of the Lofty Pines.
Well, I dreamed of the Lofty Pines—
at least what I thought they were—
standing in the forest after nighttime,
swaying so cool and sure.
Sure had never been so wrong:
sure, like the title of the perfect song.
Now for the spectacular part.
Just then, a pack of matches fell:
a logo of a tree in a heart.
They're from the Lofty Pines Motel.
All the while our dreams were our own.
All the while that didn't mean all alone.
Well, I gave the editor my pitch:
a series on our cultural wealth,
about the "error of catalogues and lists."
I call it "Why We Fight...Ourselves."
If only we had nothing to say.
If only we'd done nothing that day.
"*Je suis née pour la chaleur,*" she said,
in her Manhattan French.
"*On ne peut rien faire de la chaleur.*"
We'll just have to take that chance.
We've got world enough and time,
dreaming of the Lofty Pines.

E-mail the PM

I
We sit here on this picnic blanket
defining ourselves as plenitude to
ourselves and against our better judgment
pick up the binoculars
(the Canadian ones).
We follow the sun
to a glint
to a mirror
to the bedazzlement of a public
and find crouching panzer tanks
maintaining sweet and camouflaged peace
between ugly ideas and those who don't want them.
So we e-mail the PM.

II
Though it's easier to hold a fish
in a cloud of flies
than your attention,
everything is brand new again.
I'm hoping there's a song in here for the singer in you
working its way towards the Send button
the keyboard whispering,
"We'll give emission reduction credit
where emission reduction credit is due!"

III
Talk to him and keep your energy clean
tilt into the wind and harness its suggestion
reflect its glory; make a bird feel good.
Be funny
and transparent.
Don't fall into soft competition
between ugly ideas
and those who don't want them.
Work towards a decision so basic
it's almost frivolous
with him
the infinitely e-mailable PM.

IV
Re-enact the songs of the Cold War, be a musical force.
Sing "American Summer in the Canadian North."
Sing about Canada, even though it gets you nowhere.
Sing "You're the Man, to a Point."
Do it, or at least pursue it.

But don't choreograph violence with your voice.
You can be guileless
as guileless as a giant squid.
Be as clandestine as a blueprint
as tired as the little kid of
"Honey? Would ya go get Nana's gas mask?
They're calling for a Smog Alert."

>

Simulate a dogfight over our overrated air—
air so full of super-magnified hostility
that it lacks equity and is grossly unjust.
Air that is sinful, wicked, iniquitous.
Impress him until he declares,
"Microcosm enough!"
and
"Let the enemy not exist!"

Your PM is now
as e-mailable
as this.

Shoe Gazer

I'm wearing flip-flops
to the UN reception
because my feet
look better than
my shoes.

I Thought We Were Friends

In Montreal,
you say you crossed paths with him
every day at 5 p.m.
A slim, elegant,
tremulous Trudeau.
Every day his eyes would take you in.
No differently
than if you were Indira Gandhi
all those years ago.
With a slight smile,
as if to ask,
"Are you working on a bomb?"
he passed,
before your eyes had a chance to say
no.

Align

This fear is fear
'cause it's so new
'cause it's so near.
I think the fear is here
'cause it's so sure
and yet so unclear.
This punk is fear
fear of fraudulence
fear of reprisal fear.
O this odious fear.
I'm out of place.
I don't belong here
where poise is poise
'cause there's no trace
where there's no noise
and the vulgar choice
hard to make
harder to voice.
"What's on your mind?
We want to know
and we want you to take your time"
quickly became "Have you made up your mind?"
and in no time
"C'mon! Make up your mind!"
"Will you lay low
or will you
align?"

San Leonardo

I've seen more blurry nights than starry nights.
I've seen more TV shows than sheer delights.
You gotta get to know your cage—
the stress points, corrosion's rage,
the keeper's hours throughout the day,
his habits, weaknesses,
and stay away from the sugar.
It's not the teeth.
It's not the calories.
It's the dents in the wall
and the path worn in the carpet.

I'll tell you everything you think you should know,
unless you'd rather know something about everything.
From "the shop floor to the top floor"
you were warm to a fancy thought.

If yer freaked, we're fucked;
I love you that much.
If yer freaked, we're fucked;
I know it doesn't sound like much.

Storm Out

To almost storm out
and not storm out
life's
trembling
statecraft.

It Might Be Moot

"It might be moot
to meet today,"
you said
from a payphone
and I could hear in the background
the hissing of wet pavement
and vivid guilt—
even as I reached out to wrap you
in a Hudson's Bay blanket
tainted with measles.

I offer to be the existential hero for you.

But you've seen what entertainment clout can do.
It's an empty, drunken threat of absentia.
A punch thrown in a dream
that elicits only laughter.

The first casualty of skill?
"Mirth," I answer for you.
What follows is a silence
that is so obviously not the ocean.
A silence whose tone seems to say,
Take me off your sucker list.

"Listen," you say,
"we've got a lifetime supply of batteries
until a decision's required on this."

It might be moot
to meet today.
The day's first certainty.
Which means
another long day
of uncertainty.

Ameliasburg

Throw that bottle-green
piece of glass
back into the lake.
It's not quite ready yet,
still too edgy for your
collection.

We Split Up

We split up.
I'm on a train to Montreal,
though it could be going
anywhere now,
I suppose.

It's been coming for a while,
I suppose,
the break-up, that is.
"I've got no truck with you any more"
was how I put it.
I looked it up after—
truck, that is.

A stupid last thing to say,
I suppose.

snowy lambeau

Mystery

Somewhere there's a soccer game.
I can hear the wild crowd moan.
It's not that life here's distasteful to me
it's just that I'm all alone.
I wanted what took a lifetime to learn
and that determined then
with no more pause than a sigh
turn and start again.
It's not that it's such a mystery.
I saw it from miles away.
In time I'll only think of you
when I'm buttering my toast
or in some other reflective moment
when I expect the least
or the most.
It's not that it's such a mystery
it was practically on display.

We've got "world enough and time"
and "wither youth" comes or goes.
I hope you'll always think of me as "mine"
and not one of those.
It's not that it's such a mystery
this new-found malaise.
It's just that this mystery
has taken your place.

Vancouver Divorce

What the hell is this?
You said, "It's art, just fuckin' mirror it."
Where did we go wrong?
If not here, where do we belong?
In a shot of sun off an airplane far above her?
In the glint of the foot-burnished manhole cover?
In a light, a sign of one kind or another?
In the gleaming eye of a fighter or a lover?
Sitting here at the Hortons,
so you know this is important.
If not here, then where?
If not now, then when?
When a feather's an immovable force?
When the stampede's an obstacle course?
When Ancient Train has hit Ol' Transient Horse?
When we're a Vancouver divorce?

Now that we've hammered the last spike
and we've punched the railroad through,
thought there'd be more to say,
thought there'd be more to do.
I love your paintings—don't take your colours away.
I've grown more fearful of them every day.
Swimming up their dark rivers to discover your source,
a source of strange and unrequited remorse.
And I found the end of the world, of course,
but it's not the end of the world, of course.
It's just a Vancouver divorce.
It's just a Vancouver divorce.

Thanksgiving

Victims and their victimizers
sit down to turkey
hungry for punishment
full of mercury fulminate
serene after the screaming.
Grace makes the
mouth make shapes it's
never made before.
"We give thanks for the poetry
we read and write all day
for freeing us
to drink with impunity."
A toast to "No punishment"
replaces "Amen."
The prayer is swallowed away
to the silence
and the quiet carving.
Serene after the screaming
a little violent
but
turkey nevertheless.

Hallowe'en

The road is so hard on a schtick
and rock 'n' roll's hard on costumes
and yet each year
'round this time
kids update the ghost
do their version of a sheet with holes
the ghost brand new
the ghost evolving slowly
over time.

Gun-Free Japan

Japanese kid
somewhere in America
mistakes the night
October 30th
wrong house
rings doorbell
trick the treat?
trick on treat?
His last thoughts
were of his
bad grammar
and his choice of
esoteric costume:
a mortal husk.

Christmas Day
(for Edgar)

My dad always used to say,
just after the presents,
"Well, it's as faraway now
as it'll ever be."

I'm thinking about that as
the stewardess cracks the
public address system:
"For those sitting in Economy,
there's no music
for you today."

TV

When I was little
I thought TV was real,
but now
I know it is.

Global Warming

My friend, the Chippewa Cowboy, is in love.
He met a girl
up in the Yukon.
He says in a hundred years
it's gonna be like the South of France
up there.
He figures that he's got a bit of a "leg up" on things
with this new romance
and that this girl
is warming to the future.

Nothing but Heartache in Your Social Life

When are you thinking of disappearing?
When are you falling off the map?
When the unknown that you're fearing's
in the clearing?
When your world's gone flat?
When you're waiting for your life
to be depicted
and feeling estrangement from escape?
When you're packaged up,
beautifully scripted,
insulated with electrical tape?
When the famous are getting airborne?
When the evacuation's under way
and not for all the pot in Rosedale
could you possibly get them to stay?
When a blind eye turns to duty?
When I'm standing there holding the door,
saying things like "After you—wit before beauty"
and "OK, maybe there's room for just one more"?

When are you thinking of disappearing?
When technology fails, forever changes
and hardcore shadows are gone?
When what the average age rearranges
is forever certain?
Forever wrong?

When new adventures in electronics
make signals pleasing to the ear?
When tubes cooking up distortion
mean the end of suffering is near?
When the podium's sprouting weeds,
rendered ridiculous by the times?
When people have different needs
and time smiles on disciplined minds?
When you're getting king-sized satisfaction
in the turnstiles of the night
from all the shaky pale transactions
and all the heartache in your social life?
When are you thinking of disappearing?
When there's nothing but heartache in your social life?

Yer Possessed
(For P.)

"Go home. I'd be surprised
if you could find it with those eyes."
"Ah, go ahead and get hit by a bus."
It was the look in your eyes
when you said something like
"It's just us."

Tears streaming down my cheeks,
"Just take me to Landsdowne Street.
Fenway Park? C'mon, it's not like they keep it hid!"
It was the look in your eyes, you said,
"No one's going to hurt me like you did."
Rolling over it a thousand times
in the narrow flume of my mind.
O what I'd give for just one small caress.
It was the look in your eyes
when you said something like
"Yer possessed."
You're possessed.

Black Leotards

There's no way to get around the first day
except to just get around it.
Pale skin and wet hair stand in a tilting new uniform
on the dewy lawn of the funeral home.
She waits in the position her father left her in,
waiting for someone to come with a key.
She's resting her chin on her closely clutched clipboard
and staring out past the end of her first day into tonight
and all the way across oceans of August to September.
It makes for a beautifully vacant gaze.
Just what working part time with the dead requires—
that and black leotards.

Canada Geese

Us middle-aged men just completing
the finishing touches on a dope deal.
It's agreed; we get a small piece
in the middle of a cornfield.
When these Canada geese fly south,
we'll harvest in the dark.
We can talk just to ourselves
or we can talk just to the stars.

Us Canada geese held a meeting
in the middle of a cornfield.
It's agreed; we leave in small vees
and meet up again in the real world.
Like middle-aged men smoke dope
and talk just to their cars,
we can talk just to ourselves
or we can talk just to the stars.

Fire Escape

There's a distance between us
This early June night
on the fire escape
up three flights.
The singer in me says
Take it out on her
do anything
drop to your knees
do the midget dictator
pound the lectern blue
tell her malaria might be better
("Than the antidote?" she asks)
while gesticulating wildly to the
vast and vacant piazza.
She used to love that one.

Elaborate (Toronto #2)

I was talking to Tim.
He said you had a problem
but he wouldn't elaborate.
He was on a streetcar home
talking on his cellphone
so he couldn't elaborate.
He said, "The bad news come down."
The triple-screening or the ultrasound
didn't look so great.
He said he saw you with your guitar
and you were low.
He didn't elaborate.
He said, "Just call him, ya know,
because I can't really, ya know, elaborate."

Blackflies

So your name wasn't in the listing
or in the catalogue of lists
or in the error heavily listing.
Oh how could your name be missed?
See the bull moose
checking out another's rack.
There's no point in this.
There's no point in getting involved
when the outcome cannot miss.
No tracks in the snow, no laminar flow,
can show you "where to go"
or "how to extract just where you're at"
and not "become where you're from."
'Cause you're not quite that isolatable.
And all I'm thinking is,
I hope the blackflies don't carry me away.

Dewey Beach, Delaware

Taking turns launching songs.
Over the great bottle-green
a huge black cloud
is making assassin-aided progress
towards land.
The waves pick up their knitting.
One boy buried in sand to his chin
is pleading with his friends
who are threatening to leave him
and forget about each other.
A family of bottlenose dolphins
esses up and down and southward
in exodus.
We can hear them
when they surface
whispering in German
"auf kinder, auf."
(Get up, children, up.)

Typewriting

Past European starlings
shelves of pussy magic
and theatre fans of America
past a thousand points of interest
sacred advertising
past pageantry for the pot-head
past futuristic laundry
red-faced obligations
past Rosebud and Rorschachs
past hot-sauce runoff
and spring beyond all logic
past enzymes naïve or rusty
we are reptiles descending
in a pickled bead of water
on the coast of the earthquake-savvy
disguised and moving quickly
we are the bounty hunters
who shot Bigfoot
in the summer that hissed like Tom Verlaine.

Snowy Lambeau

Words keep like canned peaches
if they're good enough.

For instance,
"Snowy Lambeau,"
that'll keep,
and "*tomber la neige*"
(slowly falling snow),
that too,
and "tigers on the moon,"
uh-huh.
So.

Snowy Lambeau
tomber la neige
tigers on the moon

after all these years.

I would like to gratefully acknowledge the following people for their help, before, during and after the writing of this book: Laura Usher, Allan Gregg, Susan Roxborough, Jake Gold, Louise Dennys, Shelley Stertz, Paul t. brooks, Michael Adamson, Megan Oldfield, Kate Fenner, Carmen Dunjko, Bea Lorimer, Paul Langlois, Gord Sinclair, Rob Baker, John Fay and my dear mother.